Windows 10 – A Beginner's Guide

Disclaimer

Contents

Need to reset your Windows password? <u>Click here!</u>

Contents

Introduction

This book is will serve as a brief but concise guide on the latest iteration of Microsoft's flagship operating system, Windows 10. The launch of Windows 10 will remain a milestone for Microsoft as well as their millions of users across the planet for many reasons. Windows 10 is touted by the company as the last version of the Windows series.

This will essentially end a legacy that lasted for more than three decades, a legacy which started with the first version of Windows. This guide will give you a never before seen overview of the most exciting features, compatibility with existing and new hardware and other relevant information.

Additionally, the information included in this guide is by no means groundbreaking, but it is elaborate and precise. Furthermore, the information includes authentic data without any discrepancies or manipulation. The book will surely increase your knowledge and understanding pertaining to Windows 10.

So, without further ado, let's get started with the main part of the guide.

Windows 10: A Brief Introduction

Windows 10 is the latest and the most advanced version of the Windows operating systems by Microsoft. It was officially launched by the company on 29th July 2015.

Additionally, this version is also offered as an extended free upgrade for users who own a genuine licensed copy of the previous versions of Windows. Windows 10 is fully compatible with previous versions including Windows 7, Windows 8 and Windows 8.1.

Microsoft has launched a free upgrade offer for the abovementioned versions of windows operating system for one year. As per the offer, the old operating systems can be upgraded to Windows 10. Microsoft has initiated an automated activation process that requires users to sign up for a valid Microsoft account.

Once the user is signed up, this account will automatically link that account with the Windows 10 on his/her computer, essentially enabling it to download important updates and security features for free. Additionally, this process will facilitate users with the following advantages:

✓ Easier and cleaner future installation
✓ Automatic downloads for essential software and security updates

Windows 10 is available in seven different editions. Users, who own licensed versions of previous operating systems, including Windows 7, 8, and 8.1, can upgrade their system to the corresponding version of their previous system. For example, in the case of upgrades, users of licensed version of Windows 7

Ultimate will be upgraded to Windows 10 Ultimate. Keep in mind your operating system can only be upgraded to the same version and not otherwise.

Microsoft has also made Windows 10 available for users who don't own a licensed copy of old versions. This version is available as a separate CD/ DVD installation package that can be installed on any computer, Mac or other compatible hardware.

Moreover, this version is available at an attractive price and features an elaborate installation process with tutorials and a step by step automatic installation process. The ease of installation enables even novice users to install Windows 10 on their systems without any difficulty.

Minimum System Requirements

From the time it was first launched, Microsoft has maintained that Windows is designed as a user and hardware operating system. As such, all versions of Windows have followed the same pattern. Critics and gurus had criticized Windows Vista for drifting away from Microsoft's traditional approach of keeping the software hardware friendly.

However, one must not forget Windows Vista itself was a big leap away from the first OS to have featured significant hardware upgrades compared to previously released versions of the Windows series. The biggest change was the incorporation of an improved GUI that incorporated a glass interface that required 1 gigabyte of RAM and a decent graphics chip with sufficient onboard memory and pixel shader support.

Pixel shader was a revolutionary graphics technology pioneered by NVidia Corporation in 2001-02 for their GEForce 3 series of graphics cards. Their rivals ATI followed suite with their own version of pixel shaders in their then flagship model, the Radeon 8500. Other vendors such as S3 Graphics, VIA Technologies (Unichrome and Deltachrome series), Matrox (Perihelia series) and SIS technologies (Xabre series) also introduced their graphics cards with pixel shader versions with little success.

Strangely, despite the fact the pixel shader technology was available on many discrete graphics cards as well as inbuilt graphics chips for quite a while, it couldn't replace the legacy cards which lacked this feature. Cards like NVidia TNT series and ATI Rage Pro series lacked pixel shader and other advanced functions but still had enough power to run the operating system while ensuring decent performance.

By the time Windows Vista was released, most computer users were still using vintage graphics solutions. Considering this situation, Microsoft provided an option to turn off the Aero interface so the systems which had no supported hardware could still be operated. Carrying their tradition forward, Windows 10 takes advantage of its ability to detect the hardware and install the operating system accordingly. This way, the system is not overly stressed and utilizes onboard resources without hanging or restarting repeatedly.

Windows 10 comes in different versions and you are free to select the one you feel would work the best for you. Windows 10 comes in two versions, the 32bit version for less powerful systems and 64bit version for more up to date systems.

Minimum hardware requirements for successful installation on your system are:

- 1 GHz or faster Central Processing Unit (CPU)1 GB of Random Access Memory (RAM)

- Minimum of 16 GB of hard disk space

- Graphics card with Microsoft DirectX 9 compatibility (pixel shader version 1.4 or above) with WDDM driver support

- Internet access and a Microsoft account

Although there is a free downloadable version available from Microsoft and partner websites, users can still update their version during the promotional period. This will allow them to use Windows 10 without bearing any additional cost.

Furthermore, users will be able to use the software throughout its supported life. Keep in mind, you will be upgraded to the same version you had been using. This simply means if you are using Windows 10 Ultimate free version, you will only be upgraded to the Windows 10 ultimate paid and updated version.

For Windows 7 and 8 users, you may have noticed an icon appearing on your desktop. This icon is an indication your software can now be upgraded with a new version (Windows 10) via an automatically downloaded Windows Update. Once you click the icon, your request will be lined up in the queue for downloading the updates from the website.

To receive the upgrade, your OS should be up to date and is recognized by the website as a genuine Microsoft product. Users of the RT model will not be able to upgrade their Windows even if Microsoft claims so, for reasons still unknown.

Windows 10 Versions

Like its predecessors, the Windows 10 will also be available in several versions. Microsoft has chosen the "Internet of Things" style naming sequence for all versions. For mobile platform users, there is a new version called the Mobile Enterprise version.

The idea behind this version is to challenge Blackberry's sales. Both the Mobile and Mobile Enterprise versions can be installed on mobile platforms with a screen size of 6 inches or more. Keep in mind devices with bigger than 8-inch screens will not be able to run the Mobile and Mobile Enterprise versions.

From early tests, it is now known the Windows 10 mobile versions are a pleasure to use. Both these versions are not yet finalized, but still the functionality offered is topnotch. Additionally, both versions lack Internet Explorer but feature the Microsoft Edge browser app. Of all the versions, Mobile Enterprise has better support for IT administrators and technical users. There is also support for third-party apps but to what extent is not yet known.

The Windows 10 Mobile, Mobile Enterprise and Windows 10 Xbox are the versions with additional features while also having Cortana support. However, more details on these versions are hard to find yet.

The Windows 10 Home edition has a game streaming feature through which it can stream live games being played on your Xbox. It also has Cortana and

Windows Hello support which allows you to log in from your PC through a fingerprint scanning and face recognition system. Both Windows 10 Home and Windows 10 Pro are available for download as free versions.

The Windows 10 Pro supports virtualization technology through its native support courtesy the Hyper-V feature. Bitlocker is a feature for encrypting the hard disk, which is a security feature. Other interesting features in this version include the Enterprise Mode, Internet Explorer, and Remote Desktop which allows users to operate their desktops from anywhere.

It also features a unique version of Windows Store for each user which can be accessed by signing in to your Microsoft account. The assign access is a feature which locks the computer to run just one application at a time.

The Enterprise edition comes with its own unique features, including the Branch Cache for sharing your downloads with other users, connecting with VPN, and an AppLocker for apps that are listed as White List in the system. The Enterprise version comes with security updates for five years. It also offers enhanced security and connectivity features as compared to other versions of Windows 10.

Windows 10 Education is a version exclusively for colleges and universities. It can be used as standalone system or an upgrade over the Home edition. It allows organizations to integrate their PCs with that of universities and colleges, if required. Compared to Windows 8 which had just four versions, Windows 10 is a comprehensive upgrade for all users, including students and professionals as well as home enthusiasts.

Each version of Windows 10 comes equipped with Microsoft Mainstream Support till October 2020 while the extended support goes till 2025 through the Continuum features included on all Windows 10 versions.

Upgrade Your Old Windows

According to Microsoft, users are not required to enter their product activation code for initiating the clean installation process for Windows 10. However, users will be asked to enter the license code after the end of the free upgrade period. Additionally, the upgrade code can only be validated if the user owns a licensed version of a previous iteration of Windows (Windows 7 or above).

Furthermore, users will have the freedom to cleanly install their Windows without having to worry about the number of installations, facilitating ease of installation. However, as a user, you have to enter the license code to continue the installation. Failure to do so will reverse the installation process.

This means you will not be able to install Windows 10 on your system unless you enter a valid license key. Additionally, during clean installation, the Windows setup will prompt the user to sign up for an account. Keep in mind this is when the user doesn't have an existing Microsoft account. This is to ensure the copy of Windows 10 being installed is genuine and not counterfeit.

The installation process requires a bootable CD/ DVD and a Universal Serial Bus (USB) flash drive. Microsoft provides a quick guide on how to convert your simple USB flash drive into a bootable one.

Pricing

As discussed above, for Windows 7 and 8 registered users, Windows 10 will be available as a free to upgrade for the first year. This means you don't have to pay for the version after one year. Rather, you are required to upgrade your system after 2016. For Windows 7 and 8 users, the Windows 10 Home and Pro versions will be available for free provided they have valid licenses for their previous versions.

Users who don't have a registered Windows 7 or 8 versions or have versions older than these shall not be able to upgrade their systems for free. These users can buy an off the shelf copy of any of the Windows 10 versions. MSRP for Windows 10 is $119 (AU $156), and Windows 10 Pro is $199 (AU $ 262) with license. Windows 10 Home users can upgrade their existing version to the Pro version for a meager additional charge of $99.

What's New?

Historically, Microsoft remains among the most innovative companies in the IT world. Not only have they pioneered many trends in technology, their sheer commitment to their operating system is a testament of their devotion. For over two decades, they have been launching Windows series for commercial and corporate users worldwide.

When it comes to features, the new operating system takes innovation to a whole new level. Essentially, there are so many features it would be difficult to include them all in this book. Still, the book will cover some of the most important features that users will use more often.

Windows 10 is an ideal mix of new and legacy systems. This OS features touchscreen support if the required hardware is installed. If a touchscreen is already installed, the OS will automatically detect drivers from its large driver repository and complete the installation process automatically.

Microsoft has plans for launching a more far-reaching product that users could easily use and master. Like Windows 8 and 8.1, Windows 10 also takes advantage of Microsoft's innovative and user-friendly touchscreen technology. Unlike competitors, Windows 10 has a more flexible and innovative architecture that combines innovative and unique technology with legacy support.

This means you can use your old peripherals with your new operating system without any fuss or difficulty. The plug and play support has been a traditional feature of all Windows versions. This unprecedented feature is one of the landmarks of Microsoft's products.

Additionally, Windows 10 features a familiar yet innovative Start menu and Desktop. This is in conjunction with new security features to negate the need for dedicated Antivirus software. This feature is included in response to an ever-increasing demand the Microsoft support staff has been receiving for some time. Additionally, it also features a completely revamped internet browser that is simpler and more functional than its predecessors.

Despite similarities, there are certain new features as well. Firstly, you will note the system has a host of new features. Some of them are quite visible as they will be used more often. For example, the Cortana Assistant with its own version of MS Office is among such tools. This time, MS Office comes inbuilt in the

14

operating system and supports on the go editing feature. With such features, it is now possible for users to edit, modify and improve their documents and presentations on the go.

The Cortana Assistant is an intelligent software based personal assistant that was originally featured on Windows Phone 8, the mobile version of the Microsoft Windows 8 operating system. The feature has since been replaced by Bing Mobile in smartphones equipped with Windows 8 or 8.1. Keep in mind Microsoft also has plans to launch the Windows Phone 10 for smartphones, where the Bing Mobile will be retained.

Connectivity Features

Windows 10 has a host of new connectivity features while it has retained some successful features as well. There is little doubt Microsoft has tried their level best to combine new and old features from their existing operating systems, such as Windows 7 and Windows 8, but there are enough new features to call this version a proper improvement. Connectivity has been a trademark feature of all version s of Windows.

Starting from the Windows 95 internet version onwards, this feature has been quite successful overall. However, due to the arrival of much faster and lighter free to download discrete browsers, the effectiveness of Microsoft's Internet Explorer is questionable at best. So much so most users don't use the Window's native Internet Explorer to browse the internet on their Windows equipped systems, which is ironic.

Other connectivity features include a Wi-Fi hotspot feature listed under the bottom left corner. On the right side of the icon, there is a notifications icon. You can click on this icon to launch an innovative menu with buttons for Wi-Fi network and VPN. The Wi-Fi icon has a link to the network settings. From this menu, you can select proxies, data usage information or VPN. In order to access more settings, click the Win-X button.

These are the visible features. There are hidden features Windows 10 classifies as Advanced Settings. Keep in mind these are not visible and are recommended to be used by advanced users only. Another way of reaching the Network Settings is though the Control Panel, much like how it was in the legacy Windows systems.

The vintage browser is now replaced with the Edge Browser which has an elegant style and desired features. As a matter of fact, even the age-old Internet Explorer had its share of improvements over the years but nothing as comprehensive. However, the Edge browser has to face stiff competition from Mozilla Firefox and Google Chrome that are dominating the market and setting new benchmarks for functionality, speed of browsing and ease of use.

Essentially, the Edge Browser is still a work in progress but judging from what we have seen so far, it will have features such as Ad blocking, tabs and extensions for third-party apps. It allows you to scribble a note to a friend on a web page or search a phrase or term thanks to inbuilt Cortana integration. Other known features include a better user interface and fluent connectivity with more webpages in standard mode.

The Revamped Command Prompt

Perhaps the most neglected feature of previous versions of Windows, Command Prompt has finally received a much needed upgrade. Sadly, it is still a DOS inspired utility with not much scope for improvement. That is, Microsoft have done all they could to improve an occasionally used Prompt. Improvements include a flexible window that can be resized and shaped as per your convenience.

You can now use a familiar keyboard and apply copy and paste commands in the prompt screen. Keep in mind Command Prompt is still a rarely used feature only used by higher class of users and programmers but the improvements done are quite relevant and add to its functionality.

Multiple Desktop Support

Gone are the days when you had to invest in multiple systems to stay abreast with the heavy workload at work. There were times when companies were capitalizing on this deficiency of legacy computer hardware. Some of them were selling their graphics cards by marketing their multi-monitor support feature.

With Windows 10 on the market, the situation is set to change. You can run two desktops on a single display, a feature that was not possible before the arrival of Microsoft's latest operating system. Windows 10 comes with sophisticated tools and enough raw power to utilize the graphics chip's capabilities to enable native dual desktop support for the first time.

Although Microsoft has always understood the need for multiple desktops, integrating two on a single platform was never really considered till now.

Previously, in order to operate two desktops, you needed to have two separate monitors. In Windows 10, you can have two desktops on a single monitor. All you need to do is to press Alt + Tab to toggle between the apps and Windows + Control + D to move the apps between different desktops.

It is a handy feature and can prove quite helpful if you are accustomed to using multiple desktops at home or at work. Essentially, this feature enables you to run two different projects simultaneously. It can be quite handy if you are in a conference room and handling different tasks while wanting to maintain the secrecy of your work.

The Cortana Assistant

Meet the Cortana Assistant, your one-stop solution to all problems. This is how Microsoft likes to put it. However, there is little doubt Microsoft have worked hard on their Cortana app. As it stands, it serves as your organizer, your search engine, your weather guide, and your online dictionary, among other things.

Moreover, it will yell out loud if you miss any notifications, and you can use it as an organizer, e-mail assistant, and your companion in times of loneliness. Till the final Windows 10 is released, one has to believe what Microsoft has to say about it.

The Cortana Assistant is among the more notable features of Microsoft Windows 8 and 8.1. It was revealed during Microsoft BUILD Developer conference in April 2014. Designed as an artificial intelligent software assistant, the Cortana Assistant serves as a key component in Microsoft's future systems for both the desktop and smartphone segment in the consumer market.

Technically, Microsoft Cortana is an artificial intelligent software assistant designed to assist users in their daily online searches. In terms of overall performance, the Cortana Assistant is Microsoft's answer to Apple's Siri and Goggle's Google Now artificial intelligent smart assistant software for smartphones.

Microsoft has elaborate future plans for their Cortana Assistant. Although Cortana has been replaced by Bing mobile in the smartphone segment, the Windows 10 version is more sophisticated and features state of the art artificial intelligent technology available today.

Universal Windows Platform

The Universal Windows Platform is a part of Microsoft's runtime ecosystem. The feature includes revamping of runtime apps across the operating system. It also includes support for running multiple apps compatible with smartphones, tablets and game consoles. This feature enables a code sharing environment, thanks to a responsive design future.

Technically, this allows a harmonic environment that is able to connect and run many devices simultaneously. Also, through this feature, Windows 10 is able to synchronize data, such as notifications, cross-platform multiplayer games and credentials on a single platform.

It also allows developers to cross buys, where a single license purchased is applicable on all Microsoft systems for a user. For example, a Windows 10 user will be able to use the same license key for his/her Windows enabled smart devices with no extra charges at all.

Start Menu

The Start menu is among the first innovations to catch your attention. In essence, the logo and overall pattern is reminiscent of the vintage Start menu. It is the features and new GUI which get your attention. Firstly, clicking on it will reveal the list of most frequently used apps on the left side.

The tile-based appearance is almost the same as Windows 8 with few new functions. Live tiles rotate, flip and move as you keep the cursor on them for a few seconds. Additionally, you cannot add apps to the list on your left which is strange, as it was possible with older versions. Some of the apps on the Start menu don't show up despite frequently being used, which is strange.

It could be because of a bug, so nothing to worry about. History tells us Windows operating systems are among the most stable and bug free. The stability of Windows 10 is rock solid and flawless for the most part. Another important feature of the Start menu is it shows tips and tricks while the cursor is placed over an icon. Although it is not a new feature, it is somewhat different in this version of the Windows operating system.

The Aero Glass Interface

Perhaps the most popular of all GUI related features of Windows 7 was the Aero Glass interface. Guess what, the Aero Glass is back in Windows 10. This time, it is sleeker and cleaner than ever. In technical terms, the Aero Glass is nothing more than a transparency effect while you scroll, browse and explore your files and folders.

Essentially, it converts your window borders with a customized translucent effect that is quite pleasing on the eyes. Transparency can be adjusted from the Screen Settings tab where you can choose the effect with or without color effect as per your choice. Some of the transparency themes available in Windows 10 are color filled and frosted glass.

The Not So New File Explorer

Windows 10 incorporates some entirely new features, but File Explorer is not one of them. Still, there are some visible improvements and enhancements on its appearance and functionality to make it look like an improvement. Improvements include the inclusion of a Quick Access Area where you can unpin or pin the important folders you use regularly.

A more helpful feature is the appearance of your recently opened files and folders on the home screen. With this feature, users are now able to see which folder was closed recently. Furthermore, Quick Access also allows you to pin your tasks. All you need is to right click on the one you want to pin and select "Add to Quick Access" option.

Another notable thing is many icons have changed, giving you a better feel while operating your system. More file operations can be accessed via the ribbon on the top of the window instead of using the right click option, as was the case with previous Windows versions.

Unlike the previous version, Windows 10 uses the window share logo for file sharing from all apps. Now, you can choose an e-mail address straight out of File Explorer or you can add it to a zip file. File Explorer also incorporates the One

Drive, which has become an integral part of Windows 10. However, if you don't feel comfortable using it, you can dismiss it without any issues.

Windows Store and Universal Apps

One of the most interesting features in Windows 10 is now you can use Microsoft's own as well as third-party apps. Essentially, Microsoft is pushing hard for universal apps that are compatible with other platforms as well. The idea is not new but it surely has garnered enough support from within the company in recent years.

As a result, Windows 10 comes with inbuilt compatibility with many third-party apps. Microsoft is keen on promoting developers to make Windows-compatible apps in future for the sake of expansion. Is Microsoft following in Google's footprints? Perhaps not yet, but there is a possibility it will for the sake of the Windows Phone series at least.

These apps will also be compatible with their other products, such as Xbox and Windows Mobile. Windows 10 also comes bundled with universal apps. Previously, Windows 8 and its versions came preinstalled with Metro Apps. Technically, these are in addition to other desktop apps but now native and third-party apps can be found on Windows 10.

The Start menu also features Live Tiles app. Since third-party apps are trendy and popular, something Microsoft missed when they launched Windows 8. They are now trying to make up for lost ground. Essentially, they seem to be learning from the success of Android and iOS. Both platforms have accumulated

tremendous success by introducing third-party app support for their respected devices.

Microsoft is also looking to snatch or share popular app developers from all corners of the planet. There is a possibility you will not find many third-party apps even in Windows 10, but at least the ice has been melted. The Windows 10 features a new Windows Store. A lot of attention has been given to the interface and functionality. Still, not many apps are to be seen once you go through the store apart from the universal apps and a bunch of desktop apps.

There is a Google Play Store feel to the Windows Store, not because of design but the idea is pretty much the same. You can download universal as well as desktop apps from the app store. Once downloaded, the app is installed automatically without you going through the installer and stuff as was the case in previous versions.

The apps can be uninstalled with equal ease, without having to run the primitive uninstaller sequence from the usual control panel/ add remove programs, thanks to the sandbox style found on other operating systems these days. In sandboxing, the app is removed from the entire system once the uninstall button is pressed much like how universal apps work.

If that's not all, certain organizations have deployed their own versions of Windows apps and landed them in the Windows Store. The Windows Store is managed by Business Store Portal that handles the store, and manages app licenses and payments in a centralized manner.

When it comes to the quality of inbuilt apps, Windows 10 apps take the crown and rightly so. This time around, the OS has a lot to share. For example, the all new photo app offers complete functionality with a catalogue and tools for editing. The quality of this app is topnotch and rivals the Photoshop app in many departments. The quality of this app is such that despite having a Photoshop app on your computer, you may end up using this app more often instead.

The functionality of the Windows e-mail client was always questionable at best. Finally, Microsoft has sorted things out with it as it finally works the way it should. You can question the quality, however, you cannot object on its functionality this time around. The mail client in Windows 8 and 8.1 was one of the biggest shortcomings of the system. The feature list was nowhere to be seen, if there was such a thing.

Then, the questionable connectivity despite a speedy connection was another embarrassment. However, the new e-mail client in Windows 10 is on par with the Outlook client and rivals some of the better mail clients out there. There is calendar support and task tracking among others which makes the new client a nice little app that delivers the goods. The client also has live news, weather and sports feed, much like other popular email clients today. To launch these apps, you can access them from the Start menu.

Interestingly, there is a money app which lets you follow your financial and stock investments but the app needs more work as it looks like a half-baked idea with a middling performance. The results are not as desired and can be quite inaccurate at times.

However, despite tremendous improvement in the apps and third-party app department, not all is sunshine. Perhaps the worst performing app in Windows 10 is People. For starters, there aren't sufficient options, and there is questionable web based contact search function that is no way near Google Contacts or Apple's iCloud. The fact that you cannot select multiple contacts simultaneously for deleting or linking together is enough to highlight the lackluster performance of this app.

Security Features

Windows 10 comes with excellent security features for both apps as well as the operating system. These features help guard the system from all known viruses and security threats. Although Microsoft believes it is immune to them all, the reality is no operating system to date is completely immune to all security threats. Still, it is a major improvement and a welcome feature for Windows users.

Windows 10 is built upon the New Technology (NT) architecture which was designed with security as a high preference. All Windows versions from 2000 onwards are based on this architecture. There are additional security features in Windows 10, which are as follows:

Device Guard

The Microsoft Device Guard is software which blocks attacks and spoofing by applications that find vulnerability in the operating system. The feature denies

25

permission to access the system for external applications, Trojans and viruses. A lot went into the development of this application as Microsoft has teamed up with some of the most recognized names in the industry, including Fujitsu, NCR, Acer, Toshiba and Lenovo, among others. The app secures point to safe systems, Internet of Things devices, and ATM machines, among others.

Windows Hello

Touted by Microsoft as the "Password Killer", the Windows Hello employs sophisticated biometrics and algorithms similar to the way Google Now works. Furthermore, this feature also recognizes fingerprint, face, and iris to identify the user.

Microsoft Passport

The new Passport feature enables users to authenticate websites, applications, and networks. The system asks the user to have possession of the device before the process is initiated. The next step is entering the pin code in the authentication area upon which the user will get instant access to the main system, websites and networks. This tool also uses biometric sensors to work properly.

Summary

Windows 10 is the latest avatar of Microsoft's Windows series of operating systems. By default, Windows 10 uses the most advanced technology available in the world of information technology. There is little doubt Microsoft has left no stone unturned and thrown all they could to boost their OS' performance and popularity.

This version has a lot to offer but not all is sunshine with Windows 10. Their Windows Store leaves much to be desired and has fewer apps than even the Blackberry App Store. This is not enough as the rivals offer something better.

They have hundreds of thousands of apps and the count goes on. The Windows Store is open to third-party apps, as assured to Microsoft by their partners. How long it will take for them to make an impact, let's wait and watch.

If it works, the operating system could well become the leading OS for mobile and computer users. Historically, the Windows lineup of operating systems has garnered a faithful fan following around the world. Almost all departments of the OS have seen tremendous improvement but Microsoft are clever enough not to touch areas that already provided decent functionality.

Conclusion

Critics call it the ultimate mixture of Windows 7 and 8 with a tinge of new features to make it more popular among PC users and fans alike. This is the need of the hour as smartphones and tablets have taken a large chunk of personal computing from desktops and even laptops. As one of the pioneers of desktop computing, Microsoft saw the situation developing and developed the ultimate Windows version by adding flavors that are likely to please all.

Keep in mind it is too early to draw conclusions if the Windows 10 is going to be the game changer in the market. There are many reasons for it. First, the market has become so diverse it is almost impossible to predict the future of Windows 10 PC edition.

Windows Mobile 10, however, is another story as it is facing fierce rivals, such as Android and iOS. Both are pioneers of innovative smartphone trends, such as touchscreen. Windows 10 is a promising operating system that is far ahead in capabilities as compared to its predecessors. But considering the market trends, only time will tell if it proves to be a success.